J636.753 Wilcox, Charlotte.
WIL
          The greyhound.

          $21.26

LEARNING ABOUT DOGS

THE GREYHOUND

BY CHARLOTTE WILCOX

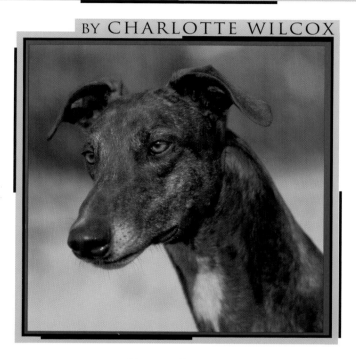

Consultant:
Robin Krautbauer
Greyhound Pets of America

CAPSTONE
HIGH-INTEREST
BOOKS

an imprint of Capstone Press
Mankato, Minnesota

Capstone High-Interest Books are published by Capstone Press
151 Good Counsel Drive, P.O. Box 669, Mankato, Minnesota 56002
http://www.capstone-press.com

Library of Congress Cataloging-in-Publication Data

Wilcox, Charlotte.
The greyhound/by Charlotte Wilcox.
    p.cm.—(Learning about dogs)
    Includes bibliographical references (p. 45) and index.
    ISBN 0-7368-0764-0
    1. Greyhounds—Juvenile literature. [1.Greyhounds. 2. Dogs. 3. Pets]
I. Title. II. Series.
SF429.G8 W56 2001
636.753'4—dc21   00-009840

Summary: Discusses the history, development, habits, uses, and care of Greyhounds.

Editorial Credits
Leah K. Pockrandt, editor; Lois Wallentine, product planning editor; Timothy Halldin,
    cover designer and illustrator; Katy Kudela, photo researcher

Photo Credits
Cheryl A. Ertelt, 10, 30
Jean M. Fogle, 15, 24, 27, 28, 34, 38
Kent and Donna Dannen, 6, 9, 12, 16, 33
Mark Raycroft, cover, 1, 4, 19, 20, 22, 37
Visuals Unlimited/Bud Nielsen, 40–41

1 2 3 4 5 6 06 05 04 03 02 01

TABLE OF CONTENTS

Quick Facts about the Greyhound

Description

Height: Greyhounds stand 25 to 30 inches (64 to 76 centimeters) tall. Height is measured from the ground to the withers. The withers are the tops of the shoulders.

Weight: Most Greyhounds weigh between 50 and 80 pounds (23 and 36 kilograms).

Physical features: Greyhounds are the world's fastest dogs. They can run as fast as 45 miles (72 kilometers) per hour. They have muscular bodies and long heads, necks, and legs. Greyhounds and other sighthounds have better eyesight than sense of smell.

Color: Greyhounds can be a variety of colors. They can be black, white, brown, and blue.

Development
Place of origin: Greyhounds came from the region bordering the Mediterranean Sea. Egypt and Greece are two of the countries in the Mediterranean region.

History of breed: Greyhounds descended from ancient hunting dogs that lived about 4,000 years ago.

Numbers: In 1999, the National Greyhound Association registered 27,059 Greyhounds. In 1999, the American Kennel Club registered 146 Greyhounds. The Canadian Kennel Club registered 20 Greyhounds in 1999. Owners who register their Greyhounds record their dogs' breeding records with an official club.

Uses: Most Greyhounds in North America begin their lives as racing dogs. Many are later adopted as pets.

CHAPTER 1

THE FASTEST DOG ON EARTH

Greyhounds are the fastest dog breed. Their long legs and slender bodies help them travel at high speeds. Greyhounds can reach speeds of 45 miles (72 kilometers) per hour. In three strides, Greyhounds can be running as fast as 30 miles (48 kilometers) per hour.

Most racing dogs are Greyhounds. Their running ability makes Greyhounds successful racing dogs. Dog racing is popular in many countries. It is especially popular in the United States and Australia. Each year, millions of people around the world attend dog races and place bets on the dogs.

Many people are surprised to learn that few Greyhounds are gray. Greyhounds come in many colors. They can be black and white or shades of brown. They can be light tan or

Greyhounds are fast runners.

dark red-brown. They can be streaked, spotted, or speckled. Few Greyhounds are gray. This color is called blue.

Speed and Sight

Greyhounds are part of a dog group called sighthounds or gazehounds. Breeds in this group hunt by sight more than smell. Other sighthound breeds include Afghans, Irish Wolfhounds, Salukis, and Whippets. Sighthounds are long and lean. They also are fast runners.

Greyhounds have good eyesight. They can see an animal move as far as one-half mile (.8 kilometer) away. They have an instinct to chase anything that moves. This inborn ability makes them good at hunting rabbits and other fast game animals.

Greyhound Shape

Greyhounds and other sighthounds have an aerodynamic shape. Their body shape causes little wind resistance. This resistance would slow down the dogs.

Greyhounds have long legs, a narrow head, a deep chest, and sloping ribs. A narrow head is less wind-resistant than a square head. Sloping

A Greyhound's body shape helps it run fast.

ribs allow Greyhounds' lungs to expand and hold more air. This lung capacity gives Greyhounds great endurance.

The shape of Greyhounds' feet also helps them run fast. A Greyhound's foot often is called a "hare's foot." It is narrow and long like a rabbit's foot. Greyhounds have long, webbed toes. The long toes allow Greyhounds to grab ahold of the ground. The webbing between their toes provides more force as Greyhounds push off to run.

CHAPTER 2

THE BEGINNINGS OF THE BREED

No one is sure where sighthound breeds began. Sighthounds are among the world's oldest types of dog. Their appearance has changed little in thousands of years. Dogs with sleek bodies and heads appear in ancient drawings, statues, and writings from the Mediterranean region. Countries that border the Mediterranean Sea make up this region.

Stories and Legends about the Breed

Sighthounds may have originally lived in Egypt. Drawings of sighthounds appear on the walls of Egyptian tombs built 3,500 years ago. The drawings show dogs hunting large game animals such as deer and antelopes. The dogs look much like modern Greyhounds. The Egyptians often drew the god Anubis in the form of a sighthound.

Greyhounds and other sighthounds may have lived in Egypt.

Many different groups of people used sighthounds throughout history.

When rich Egyptians died, their dogs were killed and made into mummies. A drying process preserved these dogs' bodies after death. The mummified dogs were buried with their owners.

Ancient Greeks also may have owned sighthounds. Greek legends describe sighthounds owned by mythical gods. *The Odyssey* is a famous legend written by the Greek poet Homer in about 800 B.C. The hero of the story was a man named Odysseus. He was away from home for many years fighting wars. When he returned home, his sighthound Argos was the only one who recognized him.

Alexander the Great was king of Macedonia from 336 to 323 B.C. Today, this region is part of Greece. Alexander took many dogs into battle. His favorite dog was a sighthound named Peritas. According to legend, Peritas attacked an elephant during a battle. The elephant killed Peritas. Alexander held a large funeral for the dog. He also named a city and built a statue in honor of Peritas.

Roman Conquests

In about 600 B.C., Romans from Italy conquered the Mediterranean region and ruled there for several hundred years. Egyptians, Arabs, Greeks, and Celts were some of the groups that lived in the region. The Celts were a large group of people who spread across Europe and western Asia in ancient times. They hunted on horseback and used sighthounds to chase hares. The Arabs lived east of the Mediterranean Sea. They called their sighthounds Salukis. These were the only dogs Arab people allowed to live with them. Arabs still use Salukis for hunting.

The Egyptians, Arabs, Greeks, and Celts all kept sighthounds. The Romans took these dogs into their homes as pets. The Romans called the dogs Celtic hounds.

About 2,000 years ago, Roman writer Ovid recorded some Roman myths. In one story, the goddess Diana gave her Celtic hound to a friend. The hound started chasing a hare. The gods did not want the dog to catch the hare. They turned both hound and hare into stone.

Ovid also wrote about the sport of coursing. People set a hare loose ahead of a pack of Celtic hounds. The dogs were rated on their ability to stay close behind the hare. Sighthounds such as Greyhounds still are used for coursing today.

An English Name

Over the next few centuries, Roman armies conquered much of Europe. They brought their sighthounds with them as they traveled. Many Europeans soon owned sighthounds.

The Romans set up army posts in countries such as France and England. Sighthounds became prized animals in these countries. The English were the first people to call sighthounds Greyhounds.

People are unsure of the origin of the Greyhound name.

No one knows exactly how the Greyhound got its name. Many people think the name came from the Old English word "grighund." This word means hunting dog. Others think the name began as grand hound or Greek hound and later became Greyhound.

Some people believe most of the original English sighthounds were gray. They think the breed was simply named for its color. Others doubt this idea because few modern Greyhounds are gray.

CHAPTER 3

THE DEVELOPMENT OF THE BREED

In time, the Romans lost control of northern Europe. The soldiers returned to Italy. But many Greyhounds remained in their new homelands.

The Middle Ages

In England, many people were poor during the Middle Ages (A.D. 500 to 1500). Most working-class people lived and worked on estates. Wealthy people of the ruling class owned these large farms. These people often kept Greyhounds. The dogs were quite valuable to these noblemen. By A.D. 1000, it was illegal to kill a Greyhound in parts of England. Noblemen hunted mostly for sport and often hosted coursing events at their estates.

It was illegal for working-class people to own Greyhounds or hunt on estate land during

Greyhounds can be many colors.

the Middle Ages. But some working-class people did not want to give up hunting or their Greyhounds. They broke the law and shared their small food supply with their dogs.

Color Changes in the Breed

The differing needs of people resulted in many Greyhound colors. Working-class people tried to hide their Greyhounds. They wanted dark-colored Greyhounds that were harder to see in the woods. These dogs were black or darker shades of tan and brown. Working-class people also bred dogs whose coats had a streaked pattern called brindle. This pattern includes shades of tan, brown, and black.

Wealthy people preferred light-colored Greyhounds. These owners wanted to easily spot lost dogs in the woods. Wealthy people developed Greyhounds that had several large white patches. Many of these dogs also had spots of black or red-brown. Some Greyhounds were ticked. This pattern is white with dark speckles.

Working-class people wanted dark-colored Greyhounds.

In time, it became legal for working-class people to own Greyhounds again. But large dogs were expensive to feed and keep. Most Greyhounds still belonged to the wealthy.

A Noble Sport

Coursing events became popular throughout England during the 1500s. Queen Elizabeth I ordered the adoption of coursing rules and standards. The race area was called a course. It was about 3 miles (4.8 kilometers) long.

Greyhounds came to North America during colonial times.

The queen's rules were much the same as today's Greyhound coursing rules in England. People let hares loose at the beginning of the course. The dogs received points for speed and how well they controlled the movements of the hare. They received additional points for tripping, catching, or killing the hare. In 1776, an English nobleman organized the first coursing club open to the public. In 1858,

Greyhound owners formed the National Coursing Club of England.

Pedigrees and Registration

The Greyhound breed's value increased along with the popularity of coursing. Greyhound breeding became a business. Breeders started to keep records of Greyhound family trees. These pedigrees showed the dog's parents, grandparents, and earlier ancestors.

In 1882, the National Coursing Club of England required that dogs be registered. Dogs could only race in public events if the club had its pedigree on file. Most of today's Greyhounds are descended from these early racing dogs.

Early American Greyhounds

Greyhounds first came to North America during colonial times. But Greyhounds were rare in North America until the mid-1800s. At that time, many people began moving west. These settlers had problems with jackrabbits and coyotes. These animals damaged settlers' crops

Volunteers find homes for many retired racing Greyhounds.

and killed their livestock. Greyhounds were good at hunting the unwanted animals.

People in North America became interested in Greyhound racing. In the late 1800s, Greyhound coursing began in North America. Coursing events are still held in western North America.

Park Coursing and Track Racing

In 1876, two new types of Greyhound events were held in England. The first event was called a park course. This fenced-in course was only 800 yards (732 meters) long. Its short length allowed more people to see the entire event. Dogs were judged on a point system similar to regular coursing.

The other event was the first Greyhound track race. Organizers set up a long, straight track. The dogs chased after a toy rabbit called a lure. But the dogs did not actually catch the moving toy. Dogs won based on how fast they chased the lure. Both park coursing and track racing were unsuccessful in England at the time.

In 1912, Owen Patrick Smith invented a mechanical lure. This motorized device moved in a circle around an oval track. In 1919, Smith opened the first dog-racing track in California. In 1926, the first dog-racing track opened in England. The sport then spread to Ireland and Australia.

CHAPTER 4

THE GREYHOUND TODAY

Oval tracks provided a new use for Greyhounds. Today, about 55 Greyhound tracks host races in the United States. More than 25 million people attend these races each year.

At the Racetrack

The length of Greyhound races varies. Tracks are one-fourth mile (.4 kilometer) long. Most races last only about 30 seconds. The shortest race is five-sixteenths mile (.5 kilometer). The longest is nine-sixteenths mile (.9 kilometer).

Greyhounds wear special clothing and equipment when they race. They wear brightly colored blankets so they can be identified. They also wear muzzles. These mouth guards are mostly used to identify dogs if a race has a photo finish. Judges then can identify the race winner on a

Racing Greyhounds may live at their owners' farms during the off-season.

25

photograph. Muzzles also protect dogs from nipping each other or causing other injuries.

The Racing Greyhound

The National Greyhound Association registered 27,059 Greyhounds in 1999. Owners register racing Greyhounds when they are track age. This age is between 14 and 17 months old.

Puppies are able to start training when they are about 8 weeks old. Greyhound puppies race each other in long pens called runs. Greyhounds learn to chase a mechanical lure when they are about 1 year old. This training lasts six to eight months.

In the past, Greyhounds were trained to chase live rabbits. Trainers allowed the dogs to kill the rabbits if they caught them. Today, most trainers use only mechanical lures.

Greyhounds begin racing at tracks when they are about 18 months old. Each young Greyhound runs in six races to start. Dogs that earn one of the top four places in a race continue to race. Dogs who do not place in the top four spots in any race do not race again.

A Racer's Life

Racing Greyhounds are graded according to their ability and experience. They always race with

Greyhounds can reach speeds of more than 40 miles (64 kilometers) per hour.

other dogs of their grade. Dogs that win many races move to a higher grade. Race dog owners receive prize money if their dogs win. The prize money varies depending on the dog's grade.

Greyhounds race for two to three years before they retire. The top racers go back to their home farms. Their owners then use them for breeding. Owners hope that these dogs will pass on their racing qualities to their puppies.

Some retired Greyhounds become family pets. Groups throughout North America find homes for

Greyhounds advance to higher grades as they win races.

retired racers. But more Greyhounds retire each year than there are people available to adopt them.

Thousands of Greyhounds retire from racing every year. In the past, most Greyhounds were euthanized before they were 5 years old. These animals were injected with substances that stopped their breathing or heartbeat. Few people thought they would make good pets. Many people believed that the dogs were mean because of the muzzles they wore during races.

The number of Greyhounds being euthanized recently has decreased. Volunteers have spent much time and effort rescuing retired race dogs. Rescue groups work to find homes for these dogs.

Pets and Show Dogs

Some Greyhounds are raised only as pets or show dogs. These Greyhounds are not involved in racing. The American Kennel Club registered 146 Greyhounds in 1999. The Canadian Kennel Club registered only 20 Greyhounds in 1999.

Show Greyhounds have different physical characteristics than racing Greyhounds. Show Greyhounds often have longer heads. Males weigh between 65 and 70 pounds (29 and 32 kilograms). Females weigh about 5 pounds (2.3 kilograms) less. The height of show Greyhounds ranges from 27 to 30 inches (69 to 76 centimeters).

Racing Greyhounds usually are smaller and more muscular than show dogs. Most racing males weigh between 65 and 85 pounds (29 and 39 kilograms). Most females weigh 15 to 20 pounds (6.8 to 9.1 kilograms) less. The height of racing Greyhounds ranges from 25 to 30 inches (64 to 76 centimeters).

CHAPTER 5

OWNING A GREYHOUND

During the 1950s, people in England recognized the good qualities of racing dogs. They adopted retired dogs from the track. Greyhound rescue groups found homes for the dogs.

This movement spread to North America during the 1980s. Today, dozens of Greyhound rescue groups work in North America. Group members pick up retired dogs at tracks. Some rescue groups operate adoption centers at the tracks. Other tracks provide information about how to adopt Greyhounds.

The Retired Greyhound

Most Greyhounds available for adoption are 2 to 5 years old. The 2-year-olds probably were poor racers or suffered injuries that prevented them from racing. The older dogs probably were

People have recognized the good qualities of retired racing Greyhounds.

talented racers. Retired racing dogs usually have some obedience training and are easy to housebreak. Most Greyhound adoptions cost $200 or less.

Racing Greyhounds usually receive good care from their owners. These dogs are used to being handled by different people. But they seldom receive much affection at the track. Most adopted Greyhounds bond well with their new owners. The dogs usually are calm and quiet. Most adopted Greyhounds live to be 12 to 14 years old.

Some Greyhounds may not be good pets for families with other animals. Greyhounds have three levels of prey drive. Dogs with a high drive cannot be trained to live with small animals. Most Greyhounds with a medium prey drive can be trained to live with cats and small dogs.

Greyhounds with low prey drive usually have little interest in chasing cats or dogs. People who adopt these Greyhounds still need to train the dogs not to play too roughly with the smaller animals. But Greyhounds may behave differently if they see small animals outside. Good adoption groups can discover the Greyhounds' prey drive prior to adoption.

Greyhounds must be kept on a leash or in a fenced yard when they are outside.

People also may adopt Greyhounds from breeders. Breeders raise Greyhounds for sale. People may find a quality breeder through a local Greyhound club or organization.

Caring for a Greyhound

Greyhounds are easier to care for than some other breeds. They are easy to control and clean up after.

Most Greyhounds seem to enjoy chasing. For this reason, owners must keep them in a fenced yard or on a leash at all times.

Greyhounds need plenty of fresh, clean water to drink each day.

Greyhounds seldom need muzzles after they leave the track. But they may need muzzles if owners enter them in coursing events. Greyhounds have very thin skin. It may tear easily if nicked by another dog's tooth during the competition.

Greyhounds have thin coats of fur and little body fat. These traits make them sensitive to cold, heat, and rain. They should not live in an outside doghouse or kennel. They should live in a home. Greyhounds should wear sweaters if they go outside in cold weather.

Feeding a Greyhound

Greyhounds are in racing condition when they leave the track. They may appear thin to their new owners. Owners can determine a Greyhound's proper weight by looking at its ribs. Owners should barely see the ribs toward the rear of the body of their dogs. Dogs are too thin if all the ribs are visible. Dogs are too heavy if owners cannot see any ribs. Greyhounds should not be overweight. This condition may cause serious health problems.

Greyhounds usually gain a few pounds after they are adopted. Most owners feed their Greyhounds 2 to 3 cups of dry kibble dog food twice per day. Kibble is good for Greyhounds' teeth and keeps their gums healthy. It is important not to feed dogs more than they need.

All dogs need plenty of fresh, clean water. They should have water available at all times. Dogs need to be able to drink when they are thirsty.

Grooming

All Greyhounds need to be groomed. Owners need to keep their dogs neat and clean. Greyhounds also clean themselves with their tongues.

Owners have a few grooming duties to keep their Greyhounds clean and healthy. Greyhounds do not shed as much as most other breeds. Their short hair does not need much grooming. Owners should use a hound glove on their dogs' coat a few times a week or daily. This coarse glove picks up the Greyhounds' loose hairs.

Greyhound owners do not need to bathe their dogs often. Owners should only bathe their dogs when they are dirty. Greyhounds' skin will become dry if owners bathe their dogs too often. The dry skin then will flake and the coat will have a dull, unhealthy appearance.

Greyhound owners must care for their dogs in other ways. Some dogs' toenails can grow too long. Owners must trim Greyhounds' nails every few weeks. Nails that are too long make a clicking sound on hard surfaces when Greyhounds walk. Veterinarians can show owners how to trim nails properly.

Greyhounds should wear a sweater or blanket when they go outside in the cold.

Greyhound owners also must care for their dogs' teeth. Greyhounds need their teeth cleaned regularly. Owners should use a special dog toothpaste and toothbrush. Owners cannot use human toothpaste on dogs because it must be spit out. Dogs cannot spit. Dogs need toothpaste they can swallow.

Owners must check and clean their Greyhounds' ears regularly. Their ears are called "rose ears" because they curl back and look like roses. Because of its shape, this type of ear is not prone

With proper care, Greyhounds can live many happy years with their families.

to ear diseases. Owners should clean their dogs' ears with a cotton ball moistened with a canine ear-cleaning solution. Owners may use a bit of baby oil if a cleaning solution is unavailable.

Medical Care

Dogs need an annual checkup to guard against diseases. At this medical exam, a veterinarian may give the dog vaccinations. Dogs need these shots of medicine every year to protect them from illness and disease. The veterinarian also may take blood samples to check if the dog has certain diseases.

Veterinarians also check Greyhounds for parasites such as heartworms, fleas, ticks, and mites. Owners can give their dogs pills to protect them from heartworms. Mosquitoes carry these tiny worms. They enter a dog's heart and slowly destroy it. Dogs also need a yearly checkup for other types of worms.

Owners must check their Greyhounds' skin for ticks every day during warm weather. Some ticks carry Lyme disease. This illness can disable or kill an animal or person. Fleas, lice, and mites are tiny insects that live on a dog's skin. Owners may use flea collars or apply medicine to their dogs to keep these insects away.

Regular visits to a veterinarian are an important part of dog ownership. Owners and veterinarians can work together to help Greyhounds live long, healthy lives.

Hindquarters

Tail

Hock

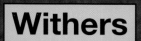
Withers

Ears

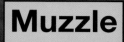
Muzzle

Chest

Forequarters

Quick Facts about Dogs

A male dog is called a dog. A female dog is called a bitch. A newborn puppy is called a whelp until it no longer needs its mother's milk. A young dog is called a puppy until it is 1 year old. A family of puppies born at one time is called a litter.

Origin: All dogs, wolves, coyotes, and dingoes descended from a single wolf-like species. People trained dogs throughout history.

Types: About 350 official dog breeds exist in the world. Dogs come in different sizes and colors. Adult dogs weigh from 2 pounds (.9 kilogram) to more than 200 pounds (91 kilograms). They range from 5 inches (13 centimeters) to 36 inches (91 centimeters) tall.

Reproduction: Most dogs mature between 6 and 18 months. Puppies are born two months after breeding. A female can have two litters per year. An average litter is three to six puppies. Litters of 15 or more puppies are possible.

Development: Whelps are born blind and deaf. Their eyes and ears open one to two weeks after birth. Whelps try to walk when they are about 2 weeks old. Their teeth begin to come in when they are about 3 weeks old.

Life span: Most dogs are fully grown at 2 years old. With good care, some dogs can live 10 years or longer.

Smell: Dogs have a strong sense of smell. It is many times stronger than a person's sense of smell. Most dogs use their noses more than their eyes and ears. They recognize people, animals, and objects just by smelling them. They may recognize smells from long distances. They also may remember smells for long periods of time.

Hearing: Dogs hear better than people do. Dogs can hear noises from long distances. They also can hear high-pitched sounds that people cannot hear.

Sight: Dogs' eyes are farther to the sides of their heads than people's eyes are. They can see twice as wide around their heads as people can. Most scientists believe that dogs can see some colors.

Touch: Dogs seem to enjoy being petted more than almost any other animal. They also can feel vibrations from approaching trains or the beginnings of earthquakes or storms.

Taste: Dogs do not have a strong sense of taste. This is partly because their sense of smell overpowers their sense of taste. This also is partly because they swallow food too quickly to taste it well. Dogs prefer certain types of foods. This may be because they like the smell of certain foods better than the smell of other foods.

Navigation: Dogs often can find their way through crowded streets or across miles of wilderness without guidance. Scientists do not fully understand this special ability.

Words to Know

ancestor (AN-sess-tur)—a member of an animal's family that lived a long time ago; an ancestor usually lived before an animal's grandparents lived.

brindle (BRIN-duhl)—hairs streaked with shades of one or two colors

euthanize (YOO-thuh-nize)—to painlessly put an animal to death by injecting it with a substance that stops its breathing or heartbeat

kennel (KEN-uhl)—a place where dogs are raised and trained

pedigree (PED-uh-gree)—a list of an animal's ancestors

register (REJ-uh-stur)—to record a dog's breeding records with an official club

To Learn More

American Kennel Club. *The Complete Dog Book for Kids.* New York: Howell Book House, 1996.

Branigan, Cynthia A. *Adopting the Racing Greyhound.* New York: Howell Book House, 1998.

Branigan, Cynthia A. *The Reign of the Greyhound: A Popular History of the Oldest Family of Dogs.* New York: Howell Book House, 1997.

Star, Nora, ed.; inception by Kari Mastrocola. *Greyhound Tales: True Stories of Rescue, Compassion and Love.* Fort Bragg, Calif.: Lost Coast Press, 1997.

You can read articles about Greyhounds in publications such as *AKC Gazette, Dog and Kennel, Dog Fancy, Dogs in Canada,* and *Dog World.*

Useful Addresses

American Kennel Club
5580 Centerview Drive
Raleigh, NC 27606

Canadian Kennel Club
89 Skyway Avenue
Suite 100
Etobicoke, ON M9W 6R4
Canada

Greyhound Club of Canada
Route 2
Princeton, ON N0J 1V0
Canada

Greyhound Pets of America
2016 S. Arlington Terrace
Springfield, MO 65804

National Greyhound Association
P.O. Box 543
Abilene, KS 67410

Internet Sites

American Kennel Club
http://www.akc.org

A Breed Apart
http://www.abap.org/framestart.htm

Canadian Kennel Club
http://www.ckc.ca

Greyhound Club of America
http://www.greyhoundclubofamerica.org

Greyhound Pets of America
http://www.greyhoundpets.org

National Greyhound Association
http://nga.jc.net/nga.htm

Index